Decorating for the Holidays

Advent through Twelfth Night

by Harold C. Cook

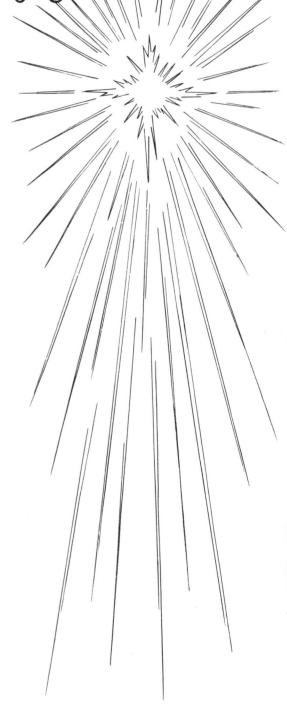

WHAT IS CHRISTMAS?

Christmas is you . . . your faith,
your hope, your love.

Christmas is a time of giving and sharing
Christmas is a time of joy and happiness
Christmas is a time of happy recollections
of Christmases past
Christmas is a time of celebration . . .
Celebrating the birth of our Christ.

Christmas is a time to express our faith,
our hope, our love.

Scan the sky on Christmas Eve and seek out
that brightest star.
That star can lead you to a beautiful Christmas.
That star will keep Christmas in your heart
always . . .

THIS IS CHRISTMAS

0-89009-480-2

CASTLE BOOKS

A Division of
BOOK SALES, INC.
110 Enterprise Avenue
Secaucus, NJ. 07094

P9-DUT-739

CONTENTS

IDEALS PUBLISHING CORP., MILWAUKEE, WIS. 53201
© COPYRIGHT MCMLXXVI, PRINTED AND BOUND IN U.S.A.

THE
ADVENT
WREATH

The use of the Advent wreath in church and family worship probably originated during the Renaissance in the Middle European countries, now Austria and Hungary. Historically, the Advent wreath is traced to pagan sources and much has been written concerning its interesting history and celebration. The making of the wreath was always a family custom. Evergreen boughs and cones from the forests, grain from the fields, nuts, fruits and berries were gathered. The circle is the symbol of eternity, while the evergreen is the oldest symbol of eternal life. Since fresh greens dry out rapidly in our ever-warm homes, thus becoming a fire hazard, today's generation makes good use of the permanent evergreens and decoratives to prepare the wreath.

Continued

On the first Sunday of Advent (the Sunday nearest to November 30th) the family prepares the wreath with the materials mentioned. A purple candle is then placed in the finished wreath, and the candle is lighted, Scriptures are read, prayers are offered, hymns are sung. Purple is a royal color and a symbol of humility and penitence. On the second Sunday another purple candle is placed in the wreath and both candles are lighted. Again the Scriptures are read, prayers offered and hymns sung. On the third Sunday a rose-colored candle is placed in the wreath, the three candles lighted, followed with Scripture reading, prayers and hymns. Rose signifies joy and happiness and is a symbol of the hope that fills this joyous season. On the fourth Sunday a purple candle is placed in the wreath and all four candles are lighted. Again the family read Scriptures, pray and sing hymns. This period of spiritual preparation reaches a climax on Christmas morning. The purple and rose candles are replaced with four red candles, signifying great joy, while in the center a tall white taper, symbolizing the Christ Child, is lighted. The white candle is then used to light each of the red candles. Once again the family read the Scriptures, offer prayers and sing joyous Christmas carols.

Oftentimes there are differences of opinion over the candle colors. True, the first candles used were white and if one prefers white candles that is the color one should use. The colored candles have been used only during the past century to add more interest and symbolism to the Advent season. Our faith is not in symbols, yet symbols, if understood, convey meaning and can enrich our worship by both their message and their beauty. Gratefully then we add the wreath to our other decorations and set our minds and hearts to the meaning of these days. In this way, Christmas means more than gifts, Santa and sparkling lights on trees. These traditions are important but they should not obscure the true significance of Christmas as represented in the Advent wreath.

INSTRUCTIONS FOR ADVENT WREATH

Shown in color on page 3

Center adventlabra on green-wrapped 12-inch straw wreath and secure with wire or florist greening pins. If adventlabra is not available use candle husks which are usually available in craft shops. Insert a shingle nail (just a bit shorter than the thickness of the wreath) through the hole in bottom of candle husk, dip tip of nail in Sobo or Velverette glue and insert into straw wreath. Space the four candle husks equally on wreath and allow glue to dry for 24 hours. Place a short individual candlestick in the center of wreath on Christmas morning to hold the white taper.

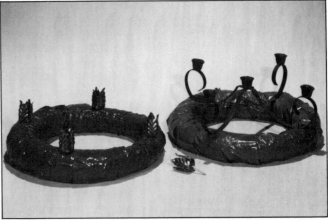

(Continued)

Pin about ten short permanent Canadian pine sprays to inner base of wreath, about twenty sprays to outer base of wreath. Pin or pick about eighteen sprays to top and sides so wreath is full. Attach 3-inch green wood florist picks to six clusters of three stems each of wheat and space equally in wreath. Wire and add picks to the cones, apples, nuts and pods. Spacing equally, add these to the wreath. The nuts and pods can be drilled and 16 or 18 gauge cloth-covered wire dipped in Velverette or Sobo glue inserted in hole. (Wormy hickory nuts already have a hole!) Use permanent cedar picks to fill in any open spaces between the decoratives and the Canadian pine. When placing picks on decoratives, be sure to hold the wood pick firmly against the stem (or stems) binding the wire around the stem (or stems) on the first 1 or 2 binds—then around the stem and pick, reserving enough wire to make one or two binds on the pick—below the stem ends. Practice several times until you have mastered this important part of designing—making sure your materials are firmly bound and secured to the pick.

I use 10-inch tapers for the outer candles and a 15-inch taper for the center candle. Since this wreath is designed with permanent materials, you will be able to enjoy it for many years. Slip the wreath into a pliofilm bag, add a few mothballs, and seal tightly with a twist tie. The mothballs will repel mice and other vermin. Store in a cool, dry place.

INSTRUCTIONS FOR NATIVITY WREATH

Shown on page 6

Remove green wrap from straw wreath. Place crèche in center base and bind to wreath with florataped wire. Cluster 6 or 8 stems of wheat heads about 6 inches long and wire with 3-inch green wired picks. Repeat same with stem ends. Insert picked heads in lower left and stems in lower right base of wreath, using enough clusters to create a sheaflike effect. Trim stem ends to proportionate length. Place grape ivy on wreath and secure with greening pins. Repeat same with individual sprays of evergreen as shown in picture. Arrange grapes on wreath and secure with greening pins or wood picks.

Cut six 4-inch lengths of #9 chartreuse ribbon and pick into loops with 3-inch wired picks. Insert between grapes at base of crèche. Cut one 34-inch length #40 brown and one 34-inch length #9 chartreuse ribbon—center #9 over #40 and loop around top of wreath. Secure with staples or pins. Cut 17-inch, 15-inch and 6-inch lengths of each color for top bow. Center chartreuse over brown and staple ends of the 17-inch and 15-inch and 6-inch lengths of each color for top bow. Center chartreuse over brown and staple ends of the 17-inch and 15-inch lengths together. Place shorter bow over larger bow and staple together. Repeat with 6-inch length for center of bow. Make a small bow of #9 brown ribbon and secure to top of wreath at base of ribbon.

Wreath can be sealed and stored in the same manner as the Advent wreath.

NATIVITY WREATH

The story of Christmas and its truly religious significance is expressed in this simple Nativity wreath made by the author several years ago. The age-old story of the Nativity remains the same today—the straw a symbol of humbleness and simplicity, the grapes and wheat representing the sacrament of the Communion, the crèche itself depicting the shepherds kneeling in humbleness at the manger on the first Christmas morning, and the rich velvet representing the kings and princes that arrived to kneel and bow at the manger twelve days later—on Twelfth Night with their gifts of gold, frankincense and myrrh.

The wreath is made of straw, bound tightly with a transparent string on a wire wreath frame. In the center is placed a natural wood color crèche depicting the first Christmas Day. A grape vine with miniature grapes is entwined on both sides of the straw wreath. At the base of the wreath and below the crèche a sheaf of wheat tied with a rich brown velvet ribbon is placed and adorned with clusters of tiny grapes. At the top is another velvet ribbon for use as a hanger in attaching the wreath to the wall.

This wreath has become a tradition in our home and hangs in the entrance hall as a greeting to all who enter. It is indeed a "contemporary tradition."

See instructions on page 5

NATIVITY SWAG

The crèche is glued to a 2x3x6 inch green Styrofoam bar. Hanger and back covering for bar are shown and explained in SWAGS, page 24. Dip pointed stem ends of natural dried cycas palm in glue and insert in Styrofoam to outline design. Length and width to be determined by space of area. A little added length and height always adds a bit of distinction to any design. Pick the wheat stems into the design as described for the Nativity wreath on page 5. The pointed star is from a collection of gift wrap decoratives and is glued to a 16 gauge clothbound or flocked wire, generally known as milliner's wire. The preserved cedar is on 3-inch wood picks inserted into the Styrofoam. Again, this can be stored from year to year.

CARE OF YOUR HOLIDAY FOLIAGES, FLOWERS AND CHRISTMAS TREE

Douglas Fir

Balsam Fir

In spite of the wide acceptance and use of man-made foliages I continue to recommend that some designs of freshly cut plant material be included in your holiday decorations. Too, I admonish you to exercise great care and judgment when using fresh materials. Make certain there is ample solution or a moisture agent available for the fresh materials to retain their natural beauty, fragrance and freshness.

Fresh evergreens add a delightful fragrance to any home during the holiday season and, if cared for properly, will last for many weeks after the other decorations have been removed. In my own home I use the permanent man-made foliages in designs where it is impossible to have the foliage stems in a solution or wetting agent. For a wetting agent I use a hydrofoam material that absorbs water. Do not confuse hydrofoam with Styrofoam. Hydrofoam absorbs water and is used as the base-holder for fresh plant material. Styrofoam will not absorb moisture and is used as a holder for other-than-fresh materials. I prefer the hydrofoam brand that is sold under the trade name of Filfast, but there are several other hydrofoam brands on the market. Cut the hydrofoam to fit the container and allow it to soak in water containing a commercial preservative until it is completely saturated. When placing the block in the container allow space around the sides of the hydrofoam so that an ample reservoir of water is constantly available for the foam to absorb. The moisture in the foam is continuously absorbed through the cells of the stems in the plant material. Many people fail to realize the importance of continually adding water to a foam-type base.

The block of foam can be secured to the container by a narrow strip of florist waterproof adhesive tape across the top of the block and adhered to the top sides of the container. I cut the block so it is an inch or two taller than the rim of the container, thus allowing the stems of the plant material to be placed at angles in the arrangement.

When using tall vases or bowls as containers it is best to fold florist wire netting into a ball or cone shape and insert it into the containers, allowing an inch or two to extend above the rim. For vases use the cone shape netting holder and fold some of the wire netting over the rim so it will hold in place and not slip to the bottom of the container. The wire holder is needed at the top of the vase to adequately support the stems.

For small stems fold the meshes close together while for large stems the meshes should be farther apart. This takes practice. Secure the ball-shaped netting holder to bowls or low containers with wires attached to three suction cups secured to the inside bottom or sides of the bowl. Wires are bound around the grooves at the top of the suction cups and the wire ends are then bound securely to the mesh holder. A few drops of glycerine or water on the suction cups pressed to the container generally anchors them securely. Three suction cups, evenly spaced, will keep the holder from rocking back and forth. Use rubber suction cups on pottery bowls—use clear plastic cups on metallic and glass surfaces. Rubber suction cups have a tendency to stain silver and other metal surfaces.

Add a preservative to the water in order to "feed" the fresh-cut plant material. There are several commercial preservatives on the market and available at flower shops and garden centers. When combining fresh flowers with evergreens or deciduous plant materials I use "Floralife," "Bloomlife" or Burpees "Everbloom." These are ready-mixed powders with full directions on each package. If these are not available make a mixture consisting of one quart lukewarm water with one teaspoon liquid Clorox (or any other liquid household bleach) plus one-half cup clear Karo or simple syrup. Use hot water for woody-stemmed plant materials and luke-warm for tender-stemmed materials, varying the degree of water with the degree of texture of the stems. As the solution is absorbed, continue to add room-temperature tap water to the containers.

When arranging freshly cut evergreens or deciduous branches I recommend a preserva-tive consisting of the above-mentioned household ingredients plus one tablespoon Green Garde micronized iron. Do not substi-tute any other iron product as the wrong product can give disastrous results. Green Garde is available at most florists or garden centers. Do NOT use the above homemade recipes with water when soaking the blocks of hydrofoam. Use only commercial preserva-tives with hydrofoam.

The popular holiday needly-type foliages include the various species of pine, balsam and fir. Hemlock and spruce are prone to needle drop even with the best of care; however, they can be used for decorations when only a few days' lasting qualities are necessary. The broadleaf evergreens generally used during the holidays are the hollies, magnolia, camellia, laurel, eucalyptus, rhododendron, boxwood, etc. Each holiday season seems to bring forth new varieties of interesting foliages to the various markets. There is a wealth of beautiful material available at this very important season, some of which is right at your door-step. Oftentimes we fail to see it until it is brought to our attention in designs created by an observing and prudent designer.

Treat your foliages the same as you treat your cut blooms. Remove the needles or leaves on the lower stems that might be directly in the solution. This will help keep the water clean and free from algae. Always give the end of the stem a fresh cut and smash the cut end of any woody-stemmed materials. Arrange immediately in the solution or hydro-foam block. It is especially important to have a fresh cut on evergreens as the pitch dries almost immediately and clogs the cells that feed the solution through the stem.

See page 44

CHRISTMAS FLOWERS

CARE OF CUT FLOWERS

The care of holiday foliages has been explained on page 10 and I will explain very briefly the care of most holiday flowers. Flowers from florists are generally pre-arranged, but there are occasions when a box of flowers is received as a gift or loose flowers are purchased to be arranged at home. Remove the flowers from the package, give the stems a fresh cut to open the cells and stand flowers in a container of room-temperature water in a cool place until ready to arrange. Use your favorite type of holder in the container in which you are going to make the arrangement. Wire netting can be folded into taller vases or meshed into a flat, round holder for bowls as shown and explained on page 9. Filfast, my favorite hydrofoam material, can be cut to desired size for nearly any type container, making sure there is plenty of reservoir space between the Filfast and container so water will always be available at the flower stems. See photo on page 9. Most florists enclose a package of commercial flower preservative with loose flowers. Add this to lukewarm water and fill container about half full, reserving balance to fill container when arrangement is completed. Lay your flowers on your worktable and separate the line or spike flowers from the form flowers. Remove any damaged foliage from stem, and give each stem end a fresh diagonal cut with a sharp knife or pruners as they are placed in the arrangement. It is best to place the line or spike flowers at the top and outside with the form flowers at the center and base. The lighter colored flowers are generally more effective at the top and outside with the deeper colors at the center and base. Place the lighter, more delicate foliages in the same manner with the darker and heavier type at the base. This method tends to create a pleasing pattern without having a top-heavy appearance to the arrangement.

Here are a few extra tips: Water temperature should be in relation to stem structure—delicate stems require mild, lukewarm water, while tough, woody stems demand hot water, varying the degree of water with the degree of texture of the stem. Use cold water when immersing flower heads, but never use cold water at the stems. Keep flowers away from drafts. If commercial flower preservative is not available use the homemade recipe on page 10. Aspirin is of no value to cut flowers.

THE HOLIDAY POINSETTIA

Now just a word about the poinsettia. Today's poinsettia plants are generally very short, branched and stocky, adapting themselves to table decorations. The clean clay pot can be left as is or slipped into a decorative cachepot. The clay pot or the slip-pots are often more appealing on a table than one decorated with bright foil and yards of ribbon. If the plant is too tall and the flowers are cut for a table arrangement, remember to sear the cut stem end to prevent bleeding. Placing the freshly cut stem in a couple of inches of rubbing alcohol for two or three minutes will stop this natural bleeding process and prolong the life of this beautiful flower. Combine the cut blooms with your favorite evergreens to create a holiday table centerpiece. Follow the previous directions given for the care of fresh flowers and evergreens.

You are working with beautiful living form and color when you create arrangements of flowers and foliages. You will find great therapy for the heart and mind when you are arranging flowers. Study the few necessary principles of flower design. Enjoy flower arranging, don't make it a drudgery!

Of course, our most popular holiday green is the Christmas tree. A Christmas tree will hold its needles and stay fresh for weeks if it is given proper care. First, select a fresh tree, preferably at a tree farm or a tree sales lot noted for top-quality fresh trees. Tree farms are often located within a few hours' drive from metropolitan areas and provide a delightful trip and day of fun for the family. Secondly, as soon as you bring the tree home, cut an inch or two off the trunk and stand it in a container of warm water in a cold place until ready to bring into the home. When ready to decorate, cut another two inches from the trunk, remove any unwanted lower branches and chop into the center of the freshly sawed trunk with a sharp adze or axe to open up more cells for absorption. Immediately place the tree into a tree holder that will contain at least a quart of solution—my tree stand holds three gallons. Have the hot solution of Clorox, syrup and Green Garde micronized iron mixed and ready to fill the reservoir of the tree holder. Brace the tree with a wire secured to a hook hidden somewhere behind the tree. A little foresight can prevent an accidental tree tipping incident. Small children sometimes become overanxious and are prone to grab and pull. Of course, your children are not so inclined! My problem is with my ever-curious large cat Cleo, always anxious to discover a way to climb the trunk, so I use several wires attached to small hooks that have been screwed into the grooves of paneling in the corner of my living room. Too, I use a plywood disk under the holder to stabilize it on my carpeting. Allow the tree to stand in this solution for at least twenty-four hours before decorating. You will note that the branches will feel soft and are much easier to decorate. Each day check the container and add room-temperature tap water.

Seems like a lot of work but the Christmas tree is probably the most important accent of your holiday decorating. You will be rewarded with long-lasting beauty by continued care of your holiday tree.

WREATHS—SWAGS—GARLANDS

Wreaths, swags and garlands will probably always be the most popular holiday decoration. History discloses that as early as 2500 B.C. the Egyptians used these as decorations for festive occasions. Restoration of the early cities and tombs of the kings revealed magnificent carvings of wreaths and garlands.

During the Renaissance (1400-1600) artists were commissioned to design floral decorations to be used in pageants and festivals. Fruits and blossoms were woven into leafy garlands to festoon the walls and vaulted ceilings of churches, castles and homes of the wealthy.

The glazed terra-cotta wreaths and garlands of the Florentine sculptor Luca Della Robbia (1400-1482) and his nephew Andrea (1435-1525) are now widely copied for holiday decorations. From these sculptured fruits, foliages and blossoms of Andrea we associate the term "Della Robbia" when we speak of the fruit-laden garlands, swags and wreaths that we use in our decorations today.

In our present Della Robbia designs we combine evergreen foliages with fruits, nuts, cones or berries. Man-made materials are widely used today due to their lasting qualities as opposed to the loss and waste expended by using fresh materials. Only top quality man-made materials should be used as a substitute for fresh materials. Properly designed, these materials are capable of creating an almost natural effect.

When designing garlands and wreaths for churches I feel it is important to use materials that have liturgical meaning. When designing for the home it is important to use materials and colors that are compatible with the area in which they are used.

(Continued on page 16)

Della Robbia Wreath

It is important to have the necessary supplies and materials in order to be able to create these three important holiday decorations (the wreath, swag, or garland):

1. Box wire frame, crimped wire ring, straw or extruded Styrofoam wreath form.
2. Styrofoam bar, 2 x 3 x 12 inches.
3. Green spool wire, #24 gauge.
4. Assorted gauges of 18-inch green florist cut wire.
5. Florist greening pins, 1 or 1¾ inch.
6. 3-inch, 4-inch and 6-inch wired green-wood florist picks.
7. Floratape, twig green, ½ inch or 1 inch.
8. Ribbon—choice of color and width.

Most of my wreaths of artificial materials are made on a straw wreath frame; however, some are bound on a wire wreath ring. Most of my wreaths of fresh materials are bound on a crimped wire wreath ring. I seldom use Styrofoam for a wreath base due to the loss of tensile strength when picks and pins are used to support the decorative materials.

When using a straw base I generally use a 10-inch up to a 16-inch diameter standard straw wreath. For an 18-inch diameter and over, I prefer the deluxe type with a hard back to help prevent sagging. Never remove the green wrap unless straw is to be exposed as part of the design. These are machine-made and available at florists, garden centers or craft shops.

Buy man-made foliages three to five inches long or cut to this length from larger branches. Sometimes one can get better mileage by purchasing the larger branches. Arrange small clusters of one, two or three stems and bind firmly to a 3-inch wired florist pick. Hold cluster firmly against wired pick, allowing one inch or more of stems to be bound to the pick.

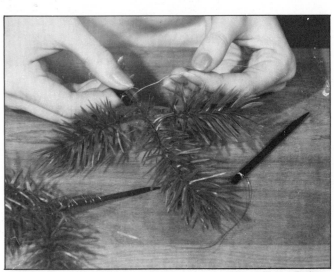

Wired Florist Pick

Bind attached wire firmly around stems only, above top of pick. Then proceed with wire, binding stems and picks, spiraling towards end of stems with last two binds on pick only. Photo shows details of this important mechanical step.

Starting at a point that will later become the center bottom of the wreath, insert picked foliages into the wreath frame with a downward slant. Continue this until half of the outer and inner circles of one side of wreath are filled. Repeat same method on opposite side.

Beginning at bottom center, pin clusters of foliages to center of wreath frame with greening pins, overlapping and covering stems of previously pinned foliages, continuing to top center. Repeat on opposite side. This will allow greens on both sides of wreath to hang downward in a natural manner.

The ribbon bow is made by holding the material firmly with thumb and forefinger, pressing the material together as the loops are formed. Start with two smaller loops and increase loop sizes until bow is of desired size and in proportion to wreath. A florataped 20 gauge wire is then drawn through the center and bound tightly to hold the bow loops. The bow can then be placed at top center by binding the wires around the wreath frame. Bind the two wire ends together to form a hanger.

After completing the basic green wreath, add your choice of decoratives by stemming them with wired wood picks and inserting through foliages into wreath frame. This is the basic method used in wreath making on a straw wreath base. The photos simplify the step-by-step method.

The wreath of fresh white pine, berried cedar and white pine cones, shown on page 19 in full color, is bound with wire on a wreath ring. Note the even downward flow of the natural foliages on each side of wreath.

The wreath of solid apples, cones and Douglas fir on page 19 combines the fresh with the permanent. Fresh apples are beautiful but not practical to use in wreathmaking. Fresh Douglas fir tips have been picked and inserted in the straw base to outline the outer and inner circles of the wreath. The large and small apples are picked into the wreath base in an alternate pattern, to maintain an effect of continuous rows. The Norway spruce cones and cone rosettes are placed at the top and the open spaces between are filled with the smaller unopened cones and fir tips. Smaller tips of Douglas fir are then picked to the wreath to fill any open spaces. A little pruning of the fir tips is oftentimes necessary to maintain a symmetrical pattern.

The open circle wreath design is often used when a decorative accessory, such as a door-knocker, becomes an important part of the design. The foliages and cones are bound with wire on a florataped crimped wreath ring. A small Styrofoam bar is secured to the wreath base and decorative materials inserted into the Styrofoam. This is designed with all permanent materials.

White Pine Wreath

Apple, Cone Wreath

The permanent holly berry, pine and cedar wreath is designed on a straw wreath base as explained on page 16. The cones are from the jack pine tree.

For a bound wreath use a crimped wire wreath ring of sufficient strength so it will not sag when completed. A plain non-crimped wreath ring should be florataped to help prevent the binding wire and foliages from slipping and turning. Although not necessary, I prefer to floratape the crimped rings as I find it easier to bind the foliages tightly to the ring. Cut the foliages in four to six inch lengths. Bind several turns of the 24 gauge spool wire to the ring and fasten securely. Hold a cluster of foliages on the ring, binding tightly to ring with binding wire. Second cluster should overlap the stems of the first. Use shorter clusters towards center of wreath, longer clusters towards outer circle so the finished wreath will have a uniform rounded appearance. Sometimes a

pruner can be used to shape the completed wreath. About every four inches lift the stem ends of the foliages and bind stems only, then rebind tightly to wreath ring. This helps prevent foliages from turning or twisting on the wreath ring. Continue binding until half is completed. Starting again at base, repeat binding opposite half until wreath is completed. Ribbon bow is secured at top with additional decoratives pre-picked and inserted into bindings. The beginner will probably find it necessary to pick clusters of foliages and insert these into the bindings back of the ribbon in order to give a well-rounded effect. Again the photos showing the various steps will help simplify the written directions. Check page 35 for details on wiring cones and pods.

Wreath making has always been one of my delights at the holiday season. When I was a boy attending high school in Princeton, Illinois, two elderly maiden neighbor ladies taught me how to make wreaths. We did not have the materials that are available today. From the banks of Bureau Creek I gathered branches of willow to form the wreath ring—volunteered to trim evergreens and hedges for the clippings—gathered cones and pods from Bryant's woods—nurserymen gave me multiflora rose hips as a substitute for holly berries. I bound these materials on the willow wreath frame with green linen florist thread, remembering how often it broke and how the ends had to be knotted together. I made them at night and then peddled them from door to door after school for a dollar apiece. People liked my wreaths. Soon I had more orders than I could fill. Little did I know that this would later lead to my start in the floral business when we moved to Dixon a week after my high school graduation. So naturally wreaths are really my first love in holiday designs.

SWAGS

Swags are easy to assemble and add a great deal of beauty and interest to the holiday scene. Again, I should emphasize that materials and decorative embellishments should be selected with care so there is a definite coordination with the decor of the area in which it is to be placed. Designs that are compatible with the kitchen are often out of character in another room, etc. Too, decoratives on swags should tell a story or carry out a certain theme. Several swags are shown that illustrate this important phase in decorating.

For interior swags I recommend using top quality man-made materials so they can be used and enjoyed over a longer period of time. Some permanent materials are available in ready-made swags with only a ribbon bow and decoratives needed to be added for color and interest.

For simple swags of evergreen, cones and ribbon to be used outdoors I generally recommend the use of freshly cut evergreens.

I usually bind branches of fresh evergreen with binding wire, using various sizes and ample pieces so the decoratives can be picked into spaces between the bound stems. Cut the fresh branches to desired lengths, laying the pieces flat on your worktable while you develop a pattern. I generally arrange two groupings, one larger than the other and place them together with the larger one below, pointing downward, and the small on top, with tips facing upward. Hold firmly in hand and bind tightly together with binding wire. Fill any open areas by inserting picked sprays into the bindings. A ribbon bow can be wired to the swag, reserving the bow wires for a hanger as shown in previous photo. Cones or other decoratives can be wired directly to the branches or wired to picks and inserted into the bindings. See page 35 for details on wiring cones.

The swag over the entrance is made on a reinforced straw base (shown on page 26). Fresh pine, fir and cones are combined with permanent apples and mistletoe. The greeter at the doorway is always in an enviable position—under the mistletoe!

The swag shown upper right is designed on a Styrofoam bar as explained on page 25. The swag above is the same design with Italian bleached wheat added. Pick the wheat into swag in same manner as shown in Nativity wreath on page 5.

Door swag at right is of long-needled pine with Sugar Pine cones and an old farm lantern added for additional interest.

Some people may find that a Styrofoam base is easier to use than the binding method. For this I recommend a 2x3x8-inch green Styrofoam bar, covering the back of bar with a soft fabric adhered to Styrofoam with Sobo or Velverette glue to prevent scratching or marring. Make a hanger with florataped or flocked wire, 9 inches long, of 16 to 18 gauge, formed into a hairpin shape, bending wire ends to form a 1½-inch hook. Coat hooked ends with Velverette glue and insert through fabric backing into Styrofoam about 3 inches down from top of bar. This will allow a 3-inch hanger to hold the swag. For added support insert glue-covered greening pins over each wire about 1 inch from top of bar. Allow 24 hours for glue to set.

Florist Greening Pins

Cut evergreens to desired lengths and insert freshly cut stem into Styrofoam. The resin from the freshly cut stem will act as an adhesive to secure the branch firmly to the Styrofoam. The stems of man-made foliages, and stems holding decoratives should be dipped in Velverette glue or tipped with a small piece of Cling (florist adhesive) before inserting into Styrofoam. This will hold the materials firmly in place. Place the longest branch into the bottom of bar, continuing around the sides with branches placed in a downward pattern, fanning outward and upward at the top. Continue to fill center of Styrofoam bar in same manner. A ribbon bow will be placed where branches merge just below top center. Attach wire stem from bow to wood pick and insert into Styrofoam base. Decoratives can then be added to complete the swag.

Completed swag for wall or door.

Wired Florist Pick

25

A Styrofoam base up to 12 inches long, as mentioned previously, is generally of sufficient strength to hold the weight of materials used in an average swag. Whenever I use exceptionally heavy decoratives I support the Styrofoam with a strip of ¼-inch plywood, width and length of Styrofoam base, glued to the back of the bar and bound with a binding wire. For a hanger I use a pull-cap from a soft drink can, secured with a small nail, screw or hot glue gun to the plywood backing. For a base longer than 12 inches, I suggest a bar made from a straw wreath, cutting the wreath, bending it flat and securing to a plywood strip. I usually drive nails about every six inches into and through the plywood strip, impaling the straw bar onto the pointed nails and binding together with a florataped wire. Prevent scratching by covering the plywood backing with a soft material. I have made long, heavy fruit and cone-laden swags on such a base.

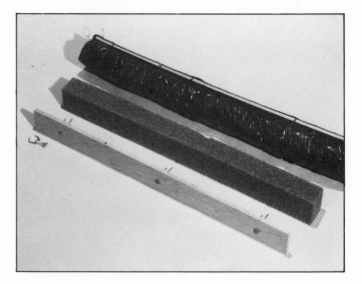

GARDENER'S SWAG

Here's a welcome gift for your gardening friend. Construct a swag, and attach a trowel and hand cultivator. Add garden gloves, flowerpot bells with acorn clappers, an Ideals houseplant book, early spring vegetable seeds and Styrofoam ladybugs. Tie all together with red bandana ribbon. To top it off for a real laugh, add a bag of thoroughbred perfumed horse manure. The manure carries the Good Horsekeeping Seal of Approval!

A hand-carved wooden shovel is decorated with a swag of foliages, cones and apples arranged in a Styrofoam base attached to the handle. Perfect for an Early American or rustic interior.

The arrangement of grain, cedar, cones and bright apples is arranged in a Styrofoam base secured to the whiffletree with florataped wires. Burlap tubing is a fitting accompaniment for the rustic setting. The old farm lantern is filled with pine-scented oil.

GARLANDS

Garlands or roping are distinctively different from swags. These are bound on a flexible base so they can be draped and festooned. In many instances it might be easier and less expensive to buy ready-made garlands and add your decoratives. However, one derives a great joy and self-satisfaction in making them. Fresh material when used outside should retain both color, fragrance and beauty for the entire Christmas season. When used inside it dries rapidly and in a few days becomes a fire hazard, especially if placed near candles, or in areas where there might be sparks from carelessly held matches or cigarettes. A coating of an aerosol spray marketed under the name of "Floraset Clear" will help retain freshness for an additional 24 to 48 hours, but that is all! Even spraying with a flameproofing material will not do much to help prolong the freshness of the interior garlands.

There are beautiful garlands of man-made materials available today. Use these for interiors and reserve your fresh garlands for exterior decorations.

Garlands of freshly cut needle or broadleaf evergreens are fun to make. Cut pieces five to eight inches long from the soft pliable stems of your plant material. Small, lightweight stems will enable the garlands to be easily draped. Use binder twine or any small soft rope, heavy enough to bear the weight and tension. The twine or cord should be a dark color so it will not show through the bindings. Darken light-colored twine by soaking in stale coffee for twenty-four hours. Allow to dry before using.

Secure the end of rope to a post or some heavy object so the rope can be drawn tightly toward you. Do not cut rope to size in advance as oftentimes the rope is shortened in the process of binding. Secure binding wire to rope. Make a small cluster of the evergreen clippings, hold cluster tightly to the rope and fasten with several binds around the rope, drawing the rope tightly towards you as you work. Keep adding clusters of greens around the rope, each time covering stems of the previously bound clusters and binding until your garland is the desired length. If the garland is to decorate a wall, mantel or outside entrance and hang down on each side, it is best to make it in two sections and join them at the center. This allows the foliages to hang gracefully in a natural manner, otherwise greens hang down on one side and face up on the other. I cannot overemphasize this fact when one is designing both wreaths and garlands.

Rubber or clear plastic suction cups are helpful in holding the wreaths, swags or garlands in position at the base or center. However, they will not entirely support heavy decorations, and are satisfactory only when used on a very smooth or glazed surface. Too, they can be used to secure very lightweight decorations to mirrors, glass or other surfaces where nails, screws or hooks cannot be used. Bind a florataped wire around the grooves at the top of the cup and attach the decoratives to this wire. Add a drop or two of glycerine to the cup before adhering to the surface on which the decoration is attached.

CONES, PODS AND MORE CONES

Collecting and arranging pods, cones, nuts and other botanicals is a fascinating yet inexpensive hobby to pursue. Start right at your doorstep and search your own area. Soon you will develop an awareness of the many beautiful and unusual art forms that nature has provided for us to use in designing arrangements of long-lasting beauty.

Mrs. Myrtle Walgreen, widow of the founder of the Walgreen drug chain, was one of my true friends. I often recall one of her quotes: "Too many look but never see." I was always infatuated by her awareness of the many forms of nature that were right at our fingertips waiting to be used. This awareness became more apparent every time I was with her. As we walked among the trees and along the garden paths at Hazelwood, their Dixon, Illinois, estate, she would constantly call my attention to the somewhat obscure wonders of nature. I began to "see." She had a great influence on my life from the time I was just out of high school until her passing a few years ago.

A hike in the country on a beautiful autumn day will reveal the wealth of beauty that nature has in store for us. Drive off the heavily traveled freeways and down an interesting country road. Stop at a friendly-looking farmhouse for permission to park your car in the barn lot. Arm yourself with shopping bags, pruners and gloves and set out on a walk down country lanes, along hedgerows and through wooded areas to gather pods, cones, nuts, seed-heads and other bits of nature's bric-a-brac. Perhaps your jaunt will take you through an old cemetery where seed pods and unusual botanical material can often be found in abundance. After a trip or two you will find yourself planning ahead for similar excursions into the countryside. It's contagious and it's good for you! Whatever your area or climatic zone there is always a wealth of material to seek out and use.

On one such trip I came home loaded with sacks of hickory nuts, walnuts and butternuts only to discover that the hickory nuts had worm holes. Just what I needed—a ready-made hole waiting for the wire to be inserted for a stem!

I gather as many local native cones and pods as I can, buying only those that I might use to add more interest, texture, color and pattern to the design.

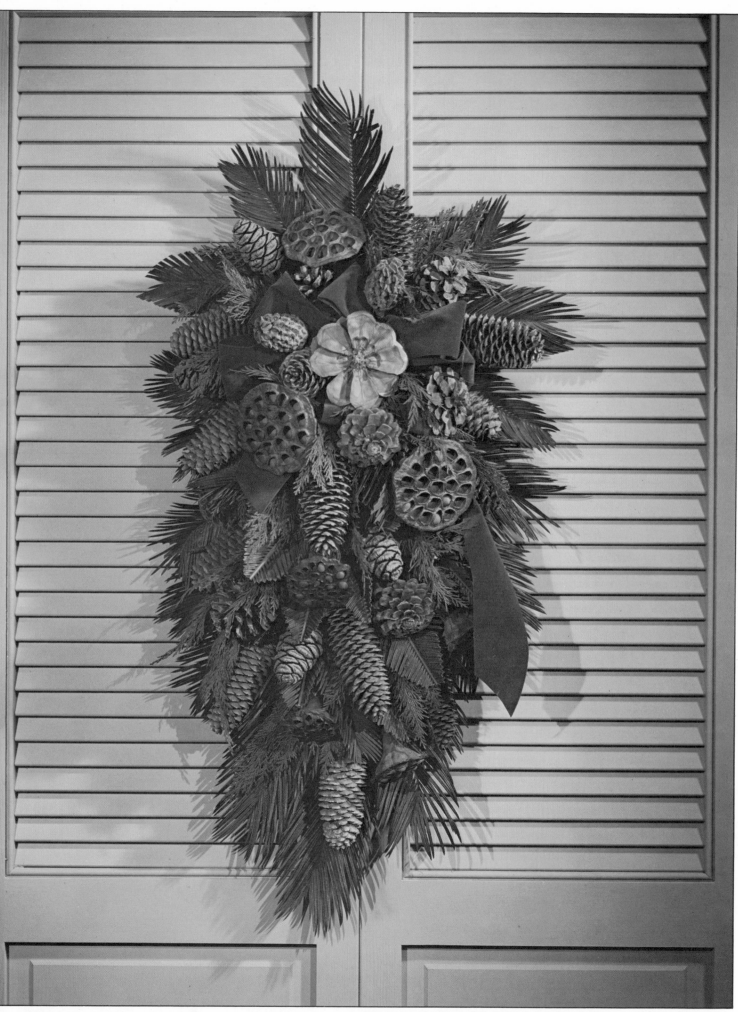

Swag of Cycas Palm, lotus pods, cones and preserved cedar

CONE IDENTIFICATION

Geographical regions, soil and weather conditions are but a few of the factors responsible for the physical characteristics of many species of cones. In a few instances I have indicated the geographical areas where the cones shown in the photographs were harvested. The size, conformation and color of the cones will vary according to regions. The words ABORTED, HARD OR CLOSED have the same meaning. These cones are handpicked before the scales (petals) open. Nature produces cone crops at irregular intervals. On the average, cone-bearing trees produce crops every three to five years, hence the reason for cone shortages during the off-crop years.

1. Norway Spruce
2. Sitka Spruce
3. Incense Cedar—"Butterfly" cone
4. Atlas Cedar
5. Hemlock (Illinois)
6. Larch (Illinois)
7. Douglas Fir (Illinois)
8. Sugar Pine (California)
9. Sugar Pine Rosette
10. Sugar Pine (hard cone—vertical sliced)
11. Sugar Pine (aborted, hard cone)
12. White Pine (Illinois)
13. White Pine (aborted, hard cone)
14. Ponderosa Pine (aborted, hard cone)
15. Ponderosa Pine (hard cone, vertical sliced)
16. Ponderosa Pine
17. Lodgepole Pine
18. Lodgepole Pine (odd-ball shape)
19. Jersey Pine
20. Jersey Pine Rosette
21. Mugho Pine
22. Loblolly Pine
23. Red Pine
24. Slash Pine
25. Jack Pine
26. Pinyon Pine
27. Pinyon Pine Rosette (reverse side)
28. Norway Pine
29. Virginia Pine
30. Sequoia Gigantea
31. Deodar

33

Wreath of dried materials

Wreath detail with cone-pod topiary tree

Cone wreath

Cone wreath detail

All the cones and pods that I have used in this book have been drilled and a wire inserted to form a stem. I prefer the flocked wire and generally use a 16 or 18 gauge, drilling a hole one gauge smaller than the wire for a tight fit. Whenever in doubt about the gauge, always use the heavier wire. Cut the wire end to form a point and dip the pointed end in Sobo or Velverette glue. Insert the glue-tipped wire in the bored hole, reserving about two inches for the stem. The depth of the drilled hole should be in proportion to the size and weight of the cone or pod. You must use your own judgment. At this stage of preparation I place the cones and pods in a foil-lined shallow pan and put them in the oven to dry. I start with a cold oven (not preheated) set at 150°, and heat them for an hour or two. Then I turn off the heat and let them cool down in the oven. This not only dries the glued stem and any pitch in the cones but also cremates any little creatures that might be sheltered within.

When working with small delicate cones and pods that do not have a center structure suitable for drilling, it is necessary to stem them by securing a hairpin-shaped wire around and through the second or third row of base petals, pulling it very tight and twisting the two wire ends to form a stem. I vary the gauge of wire with the degree of texture of the cone or pod. Now it becomes necessary to add a wood pick so it can be inserted securely to the design base.

All of my wreaths of cones, pods and other botanicals are designed on a straw wreath base. Straw wreaths over 16 or 18 inches in diameter are reinforced on the back to keep them from sagging. You may either cut a doughnut shaped hardboard to size or form a very heavy wire ring and attach it to the straw wreath form with binding wire. Bases for swags are outlined on page 26.

When making symmetrical twin designs it is best to first sort and divide the materials you are using into two equal groups according to size, texture, color and form. On wreaths or swags I place my important or key materials first and use the smaller materials for filler.

The design bases are covered with natural green sheet moss, pinned to the straw base with florist greening pins. This shields the natural straw or the green covering and gives a more professional appearance to the completed design. The wire stems of the cones or pods are then dipped in the Sobo or Velverette glue and inserted through the moss into the straw base.

First, outline the inner and outer circles of the wreath. Next, arrange the key materials then fill between with the smaller materials.

MINIATURE WREATHS IN SHADOW BOXES

Small cones, pods, nuts, etc., are glued to a wreath-shaped cardboard cut to the desired size. Mount finished wreath on your choice of background and place in a shadow box, glass-covered frame. Kathy Sherman from Dixon, Illinois, designed these wreaths and her husband, Tom, made the frames in his home workshop. Great therapy for a husband and wife team!

Swag of cones, pods and cedar

Follow the same procedure for swags: first, outline; second, key materials; and third, filler, placing the materials as if you were weaving a tapestry.

Just a word regarding bows or ribbons on designs of natural materials. If you must have ribbon use soft, muted shades of beige, greens, browns in burlap or soft velvet. Rope, braided binder twine or old hawsers are interesting additions—depending, of course, on where the finished design will be placed.

For interesting open cone flowers cut the cone horizontally with a sharp pruner or hacksaw. To make rosettes, saw unopened cones horizontally and as they open they will take the shape of a rosette. It takes practice to determine exactly how much to saw off the closed cones. If your cones are open place them in a bucket of warm water and cut with a band saw while they are closed. Place in 100° oven and as they dry they will open in the form of a rosette.

Fascinating designs are found in the structures of cones when they have been sliced vertically. These should be cut with a band saw by someone knowledgeable in handling such a tool. I take my cones to a mill for vertical slicing. It is costlier, but cheaper than losing a finger. You will discover untold beauty in the heretofore unseen structural design of these vertically sliced cones. Remember, they were designed by the greatest Architect!

Designs of cones and pods are not strictly related to Christmas decorating. They can be used in autumn and enjoyed through the holidays, but should be removed and stored prior to the Lenten season.

There is a wealth of available dried material that can be combined with cones and pods to create an almost endless number of decorative designs.

38

MANTELS

The fireplace is always an architectural feature of the room and the mantel and the wall above the mantel offer almost unlimited decorating possibilities. Here is your opportunity to create the ultimate in design to reflect your holiday theme.

Glowing embers or a crackling fire always adds a festive setting to the holiday scene. White birch logs with a branch or two of pine tied with a red velvet bow is a decorative addition to some of the older bricked-in fireplaces or where fires are impractical.

If your home does not have a real fireplace you can install an imitation fireplace for the holiday season. There are well-designed fireplaces available with electric logs that glow like real flames. And in homes without either the real or imitation fireplaces, an interesting design can be created on a console table placed against a wall.

Mantels with a mirror back should be treated with heavy, bold materials as a contrast to the reflections that might show in the mirror. Oftentimes a slight tip of the mirror will help eliminate some unwanted reflections. Mantel-to-ceiling mirrors that are secured to the wall can be decorated with lightweight garlands held by clear plastic suction cups. A drop of glycerine will generally hold the suction cup if the decorations are not too heavy.

The mantels shown on the opposite page and on page 58 are designed with accessories I have used at my annual October Christmas decorating programs.

A red brick wall is a perfect foil for the permanent wreath of cedar, pine, mistletoe, apples and cones. This particular wreath is made on a 24-inch reinforced straw wreath base. Materials are picked into the frame as described on page 16. Random lengths of red tapers are inserted into the copper candle mold. Evergreens in the basket are kept fresh in a liner that contains Filfast. The bright red fresh apples are held in position by placing in the homemade apple husks. The family will suddenly take a liking to apples when they are so temptingly arranged and a part of your decorative scheme! No problem replacing them; just place fresh ones on the husk when they need replenishing. The husk is also shown on page 43.

The hand-painted, molded Madonna plaque is centered on a white wood-paneled wall. The arborvitae garland is permanent and will not have to be replaced during the holiday season. Gold-painted Norway spruce cones are placed on fresh arborvitae on the mantel. When the arborvitae on the mantel dries it can easily be replaced with fresh greens. Avoid allowing it to become dry and hazardous. The angel band figurines are handmade in Italy and are copies of the originals that were made by the monks in an Italian monastery.

A good example of following a theme in decorating is shown in the open wreath design for the door on page 18 which is repeated on this mantel. The wreath is made as outlined on page 18, secured to the back of a Styrofoam base. The two-inch column candles are held in plastic candle bases designed to be used on Styrofoam. Foliages are inserted into the Styrofoam base. The gold-sprayed Norway spruce cones are then picked through the foliages into the Styrofoam base. Three large cone flowers made from the sugar pine cones are sprayed with gold paint and add a point of interest to the center base of the arrangement. This design can also be used effectively as an arrangement for a console table or as a background for a buffet serving table.

TABLE ARRANGEMENTS

Perhaps this would be the appropriate place and time for me to mention a very important phase of decorating—do not overdo or clutter. A few distinctive and well-placed arrangements will create a more striking effect than many little unimportant decoratives placed in a helter-skelter manner throughout the room.

Several years ago I was a guest at a Christmas party where the hostess really overextended her decorating ability. The entrance, the fireplace and her oversized coffee table were beautifully decorated. Her dining table and buffet were elegant. Then she ruined the effect by placing a holly-pine-ribbon bedecked candlestick and candle on every conceivable vacant tabletop, adding a spray of ribbon-drenched evergreen over every picture, mirror and wall sconce. It appeared that she had bought too much evergreen and much too much ribbon and felt she had to use it all in the two important entertaining rooms. It was difficult for me to restrain myself, but I did!

Select a theme for your holiday decorations and carry this decorative theme throughout the house. The coffee table is a key accent for table decorations in the living room. The arrangement should be low and designed so one looks down into it. The base should be heavy, so that it cannot tip easily, or designed with materials that give an appearance of bottom weight. A striking arrangement with an appropriate accessory is ample for the average coffee table, leaving space for easy functioning of this important piece of furniture.

The table is probably the most important accent in the dining room. A beautiful table begins with the cloth, traditionally white or ivory; however, handsome colored cloths should not be overlooked. The old damask and linens are elegant and should be used on important occasions even if it means extra work in the laundry department. Consider all the elements before decorating—the wall, drapery and carpet colors, period of design, area and table size, tabletop accessories, plus your way of life. From here we choose the decorations, picking up the theme in either color or texture. This is one season when decorations and color are rampant and the dining table is one place where you can be liberal in the use of color and texture. Work from these and you should be able to create a charming yet elegant table, aglow with the personality within the home.

Console tables, buffets and other important tabletops should be treated in a simple, yet distinctive manner. Candleglow adds much but don't overdo it. Cluster the candles in groups as accents rather than using them singly. Oftentimes the scented candles are overwhelming, especially when used in great abundance. Simmer some spices in a saucepan on the kitchen stove and let their fragrance permeate through the house. Never leave any area where candles are burning. If retiring to another area of the home after dining be sure that either the burning candles are extinguished or a family member is assigned to keep a watchful eye on them. A fire is a horrible thing and doubly so during the holidays!

See page 44

The table arrangements I have made for this book are varied. Some are simple, some are elegant. Some are made of fresh materials, some of dried, and some of permanent man-made materials. The accessories are from my cupboards. All of them, with the exception of the silver candelabra, reflect my way of life and are compatible with the interior of my home.

Candles glow in hobnail vigil lights placed in an antique silver caster from which the condiment bottles have been removed. The arrangement is made on a two-inch Styrofoam disk, cut just a trifle larger than the base of the caster. Permanent (plastic) materials are combined with cones and pods in a wreath-like design. Dip the stem ends in Sobo or Velverette glue before inserting as sometimes they do not adhere securely to the foam base. Be sure to use votive candles as coffee-warmer candles are too hot and will crack the votives. This type of arrangement has been used on my dining room table for many years.

For the home with a rural atmosphere I have replaced the silver caster with an old farm lantern and used a patterned cloth, which is especially suitable for the breakfast table. Fill the lantern with pine-scented oil and there will be a delightful fragrance.

A low fruit basket is the container for the arrangement of greens and apples. If you are using permanent foliages use a moss-covered Styrofoam base secured with wires or Plas-ties through the wicker meshes. For fresh foliages use Filfast in a liner to fit the basket. Secure the Filfast with a strip of tape across the top adhered to the edges of the bowl. The apples are resting on a wire husk made of florataped wire and picked into the foam. The apples can be removed from the arrangement and replaced with new ones.

The apple-pineapple cone arrangement is an adaptation from the Williamsburg era. Either fresh or permanent fruit can be used. I find the green Styrofoam cone-shaped base much easier and less expensive than a wood-with-nails base. Glue sheet moss to the base. Starting at the top, secure the pineapple and then secure the apples in rows around the cone, filling between them with foliage. A four-inch florist pick inserted in the fruit will make a stem that can be inserted in the cone. I use an ice pick to make a hole in permanent fruit for the wooden pick. Permanent or fresh greens can be used to fill the open areas between the fruit and around the base. This arrangement shows permanent boxwood. Pineapples are a symbol of hospitality and should be at the finial. If the apples are not compatible with your color scheme, use other fruits.

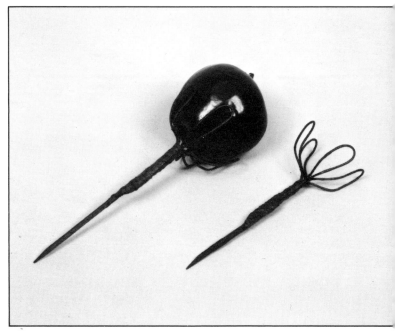

Wire Husk

Preserved eucalyptus combined with fresh evergreens, holly and stemmed Italian sabulosum pinecones are arranged in Filfast secured to a crystal bowl on a silver stand, shown on page 11. Fresh flowers can be added from time to time. The fresh evergreens will retain their beauty as long as you keep adding water to the Filfast.

The fresh red carnations and evergreens are arranged in Filfast secured to a glass epergne atop the candelabra. A daily addition of water in the epergne will keep the flowers fresh for several days, and the foliage fresh for weeks. Design the foliage arrangement first and then add the fresh flowers. Remove the flowers when faded and continue to enjoy the foliages for a long time. If your budget will not allow many carnations add a few stemmed 30 or 40 millimeter red metallic ornaments for interest. Even cones will be festive with the red carnations.

The fruit arrangement shown on page 46 with the tapers is made on Styrofoam adhered to a plywood base. The candles are held in the new plastic taper holders which have been inserted in the Styrofoam. The Styrofoam is moss covered, the key fruits and cones are placed and the smaller fruits, holly, pine and clusters of baby's breath are added as filler. This same arrangement is shown on page 41 with the tapers removed and placed between two Williamsburg-style glass hurricane shades covering candles in brass candlesticks. Fresh flowers were seldom, if ever, used to decorate holiday tables during the colonial period. Fruit was abundant and used for decoration first, then as food before becoming overripe.

Red carnations, fir and cones are arranged in a glass epergne which is adaptable atop a three-branch candelabra or a low candlestick. Allow ample room for water between the edges of epergne and block of Filfast.

The permanent holly with gold-painted cones is placed directly on the damask cloth. A ribbon of Saran or clear plastic, placed under the fresh foliage, will prevent pitch or sap from staining fabrics or tabletops.

Fresh flowers can be added as shown in the pewter bowl in the table arrangement above.

See page 44

FOR THE STARRY-EYED SET

One of the most beautifully written answers to every child's question, "Is there really a Santa Claus?" is the answer given to eight-year-old Virginia O'Hanlon by Francis P. Church, editor of the *New York Sun* in September, 1897. The answer to this ponderous question, for every child and grown-up, came in a Christmas editorial classic, "Yes, Virginia, there is a Santa Claus." This answer, which will live forever in the hearts of all who read it, expresses the true meaning of Christmas. I read this many years ago when I was in high school and have always considered it a part of my Christmas season. Yes, Mr. Church, even today, past the sixty mark, I believe in your answer that "there is a Santa Claus." Perhaps, I am slightly biased in the beauty of this editorial as I have a sister named Virginia and often recall our childhood when I did not want her to discover and be brokenhearted to find that Santa was merely a symbol.

To children everywhere this is a season of gifts, baubles, glittering lights and "stockings hung by the chimney with care." May it always be this way for everyone from childhood to old age—may this season of Santa Claus, a symbol of sharing, ever reign within our hearts.

Children love the baubles and the glittery decorations that help make Christmas. Children love to share in the joy of making these decorations and especially creating something that is truly their own. To watch children design and make ornaments for the tree, cards to send their friends, decorations for their room and gifts for their friends is an important and appealing part of Christmas.

A small Nativity wreath for the child's own room will be a constant reminder of the meaning of Christmas. The Advent wreath and the religious Advent calendar with each day of Advent suggesting the reading of a particular passage from the Bible, will instill in the heart and mind of the child that there is much more to Christmas than mere baubles, gifts and cards.

A few suggestions . . . perhaps a door decoration for the child's bedroom using a snowman with his or her enlarged photo as the face—a wreath with pixies or dwarfs—a swag with angels pulling the ropes of a musical bell over the child's bed—an old-fashioned sled with greens and berries and ribbons and real apples to eat, or a popcorn snowman, complete with corn popper filled with popcorn and draped with garlands of popcorn. And we can't forget the Christmas counting ribbon! These are just a few of the many suggestions that can strike the keynote of your home decorations where children or grandchildren abound during the holidays. Many suggestions for these decorations are shown, along with the mechanics involved in making them.

Of course, the Christmas tree stands supreme and the children should have a big part in its decoration. Each year why not give one particularly fine ornament that can become a tradition and a heritage to the child. A small tree in the child's own room can be decorated with handmade ornaments, if these will not fit into the decor of the room where the family tree will stand. Tiny lights and especially the tiny clip-on candle lights are so nostalgic of Christmases past.

I still remember my first Christmas tree. It was an artificial tree about two feet tall with branches that unfolded from its trunk. We were living in Chicago and Grandpa Cook took me to a little variety store on West Madison Street near Ogden where I selected this tree. I was four years old and it still is a vivid memory. At the end of each branch was a holder to contain a tiny candle. Nearly every evening, if I had been a good boy, I was allowed to light the candles. The next day we would return to the store to buy more candles and sometimes I was allowed to select a new ornament—so I tried extra hard to be on my best behavior! My first ornament was a glass icicle which I hung on the tree each Christmas until a few years ago, when it suddenly broke into a thousand pieces. I was sad—I felt I had lost a friend! There was a glass French horn that would play, foil-covered chocolate Santas on a string, a balloon ascension ornament with lots of tinsel cords. We made popcorn and cranberry garlands, and a tinsel star topped the tree. How I love to recall those child-hood days!

Have a special theme for a children's holiday party and follow this theme in the decorations and favors. Snowmen, Mr. and Mrs. Santa, angels, reindeer with sleighs, pixies or Santa's helpers, and especially the not-overused Little Drummer Boy are but a few of the many ideas that can be incorporated into this important holiday activity for the children. Start early on your planning and designing so you enjoy it and are not crowding everything into the last few days. Enjoy doing it, don't make it a last minute hassle!

The snowman design is cut from Styrofoam. Shoes, buttons, cuffs and hat are separate pieces, sprayed black, and glued to the snowman. The hat is trimmed with a band of red velvet ribbon. Gloves and scarf are cut out of red felt and attached. Large yarn ball tassels can be bought or handmade. The photo of the child's head is enlarged, cut to size and glued to Styrofoam.

Here's a reproduction of an old-fashioned box sled. The sides could be stenciled. Permanent greens are arranged in a Styrofoam base. Encourage the children to eat the apples and replace fresh ones on the apple husks which are described on page 43.

CHRISTMAS WITH THE THREE BEARS

The little chalet-type frame can be purchased at most craft shops or made in a home workshop. Cone petals from discarded cones become shingles when glued to the roof. Twisted chenille or pipe cleaners give the smoke effect from the chimney. Tiny dwarfs are at the entrance of the chalet, trimming the outside tree, while the three bears are enjoying their porridge and keeping warm near the potbellied stove. Little mice are enjoying their Christmas cheese in the attic. Let your imagination run wild when creating a fantasy design and always have a tall tale ready to go along with it.

SANTA BOOT

The plush boot has a liner filled with Styrofoam to hold permanent holiday foliages. The happy little pixies are secured with picks inserted through the foliages into the Styrofoam. Sand placed under Styrofoam in liner will add weight to prevent tipping. Use your own individual taste in decorating articles similar to those in this book with your choice of materials.

A Styrofoam birdcage form placed on a 2- x 6-inch Styrofoam disk is the basic structure for this design. Center cutout area has a peppermint pole with tiny Santa figurines. The windowlike openings are edged with self-adhesive braid. Outer poles are cutoff plastic candy canes. Tiny figurines of children are glued on the four small white reindeer. Miniature holly clusters are glued between the deer to the floor of the red felt-covered base. Red felt is cut to size and glued to the roof of birdcage form and around outer edge of base. Peppermint striped ribbon and sequins decorate the top and sides. A small music box with a turntable key is inserted and glued in a hole cut to size in center of the base Styrofoam disc. The music box is wound by winding the turntable. As it unwinds the music plays and the carousel revolves. Use a Christmas tune, not a carol. Reserve the carols for designs with a religious theme.

MUSICAL CAROUSEL

COUNTING RIBBON

Ribbon streamer is a #40 velvet florist ribbon 28 inches long. Candies are tied to ribbons or yarn pulled through holes punched in streamer. Candies may be covered with foil or Saran Wrap for easier attachment. Avoid giving children hard candies just before bedtime. Make a separate ribbon for each child or cluster candies on one ribbon for two or more children. Attach a bell at the bottom and sew or glue a printed poem at the top.

December first till Christmas
Is the longest time of the year,
For it seems to take forever
For old Santa to appear.

How many days to Christmas?
Here's an easy way to count,
For this ribbon filled with candy
Will tell you the right amount.

Untie one candy every night
And pretty soon you'll tell
That Christmas Eve is really here
By the time you reach the bell.

The permanent arrangement of foliages, Christmas roses, bells and angels, is quite appropriate for a girl's room, whether placed above the bed or at the mirror top. All the materials are inserted in a Styrofoam base. The clappers are stemmed ornaments inserted through the top center of bells. The center wire in the gold metallic tubing gives support to various twists and loops of tubing.

Popcorn is glued with Velverette glue to a 4" and a 6" Styrofoam ball, which have been previously pegged and glued together to form the body of the snowman. The hat is made by gluing a doughnut-shaped cardboard to a paper cup, painting it black and trimming with ribbon and braid. Felt cutouts form the eyes, nose, mouth, earmuffs, buttons, scarf and gloves. A Styrofoam bar is adhered with florist clay (Cling) to top side of popper and wired to handle. Decoratives are picked to Styrofoam. Florataped wire is secured to popper handle for hanging.

Popcorn is easier to string if it has been placed in an uncovered container in the refrigerator for 48 hours.

Moss-covered Styrofoam, edged with burlap and self-adhesive braid, is the base for these childlike figurines depicting the Nativity scene. The palm trees are made by binding cotton to a heavy wire (a coat hanger is ideal) and covering it with twig green or brown floratape. 1" Styrofoam balls, sprayed brown, are impaled and glued on the ends of wires and allowed to dry for 24 hours. Natural dried cycas leaves are cut to size and inserted in Styrofoam ball to form tree head. For a more natural look, use a pinking shears when trimming cycas foliage. Dip stem end of cycas in glue before inserting in Styrofoam. Adhere trees in Styrofoam base with Cling or glue. Dowels are inserted in base to prevent figurines from tipping. Small clusters of dried flowers are added to complete the design.

DESIGNS FROM DISCARDS

I should have been a junk dealer but I wasn't. My paternal grandparents saved everything and I must have inherited this trait from them!

We were living in Galesburg during my grade school years and Saturdays were always exciting days when I could go to an auction with my grandparents. I was fascinated by the chant of the auctioneer and the hundreds of articles that were being sold. Somehow I always managed to tote something home. And I still do! There's a wealth of Americana available at auctions, rummage sales and flea markets. One of my best sources of old discards is the material left at curbs for the trash collector, especially during the annual community spring clean-up days. Armed with crowbar, saw and hammer I make my early morning rounds up and down the streets retrieving other peoples' trash from the curbside. In a few hours my station wagon is full and I'm on my way home with all my treasures.

And now for a few of the trash items that have been recycled into decoratives. These designs are shown in the accompanying photographs.

An old rusty ladle was cleaned and painted. Styrofoam attached to the ladle cup holds the decoratives and checked ribbon. This is fine for a kitchen door or wall for any season of the year.

A useful water-holding container to carry to the garden for flower gathering is made from coffee or other tin cans welded together with a T-shaped metal rod handle. The four varied sizes of cans are adaptable to the various lengths of flowers and foliages. Paint this a bright color, place a bow with spray of pine on the handle, fill the cans with small potted plants and you have a welcome gift for one of your gardening friends.

CANDLESTICKS

Curbside trash piles often contain old tables with a decorative leg or two that can be made into interesting candlesticks. Discarded upholstered furniture also has legs that make ideal bases for the column candles. The newel-post and balusters removed from an old staircase are real treasures. If some of the balusters are damaged they can generally be cut so at least part of the spindle is useable. After cleaning, a base can be added and then refinished to your taste. A candle-cup is attached to the top. Presto, you have a group of inexpensive candlesticks! Old, discarded table lamps are another source for interesting candleholders. A footed ashtray can be recycled into a decorative stand to support one of the large column candles. When my brother-in-law stopped smoking I retrieved one of these from their curbside trash pile, recycled it into a decorative candlestand and sold it! Be alert to the vast number of throwaways that can be recycled into veritable treasures.

This newel-post was retrieved from the staircase of an old home which was being demolished. A base was attached and a translucent globe rests on top with a votive light inserted in the center. A grouping of pine, grapes and velvet fruit is bound in a ring around the newel top. The antique gold velvet tubing, with metallic gold tassels, adds the final touch for a floor candleholder.

A figurine of St. Francis with the birds has been placed on a slate tile. The woodsey arrangement is made in a base of moss-covered Styrofoam secured to the tile with Cling. Cork bark euonymus (Euonymus alatus), roadside weed stems and grasses are combined with lotus pods and dried goldenrod in the arrangement. The candleholders are made from spindles taken from a discarded staircase and attached to a wooden base. Metal candle cups are screwed to the spindles.

An Ivory liquid soap bottle is the base for the heavenly angel made of #40 white velvet florist ribbon. The skirt, arms, tunic and wings are trimmed with gold self-adhesive braid, and the sash is narrow metallic gold tubing. The angel head is available at most craft shops.

A discarded Renuzit container is the form for the little tree. Trim as you like with your choice of materials.

The little angel head is glued to the inverted top half of a decorated L'Eggs pantyhose container. The head can be purchased or made from a painted large wooden bead, using yarn for the hair.

Bottle-cap centers are felt-lined, edges dipped in glue and then dipped in glitter dust. Tiny ornaments are glued to the felt-lined caps. Caps are then glued to felt-covered cardboard in a geometric tree pattern. A gold metallic dimensional star tops the tree. Gold self-adhesive braid completes the frame.

The flowerpot compote is a simple container to assemble. Saucer and inverted pot are thoroughly scoured, dried, glued together and spray painted. A Styrofoam disk is secured to saucer and a hurricane candle holder base is inserted into Styrofoam to hold candle and shade. A holly candle ring is pinned around the shade to the Styrofoam base. A narrow band of ribbon is glued to outer rim of saucer and edge of flower pot to cover alkaline stains. For fresh flowers or foliages use a disk of Filfast but first line the saucer with several coats of varnish to prevent moisture from seeping through the porous clay saucer.

A toy broom, a ball of twine, a plastic place mat, bells attached to chenille stems, small blue metallic bells pinned to twine and a taper-size candle ring are combined to create an angel-broom for the entranceway. Be an angel and brush the snow from your shoes!

Photo Flash Cubes

Feed store scoop   Milk carton lantern   Chair leg candlestick

Spoon flowers

54

Photo flash cubes can be decorated with scenes on the inside as well as the outside. Leave cube intact if the decorations are to be on the outside of cube. Adhere decoratives with Sobo or Velverette glue, creating your individual designs on the top, bottom and sides of cube. In the photograph, four designs are shown with solid decoratives on all sides. One cube is sprayed silver and trimmed with pieces of discarded jewelry. Another is sprayed with bronze paint and the sides of cube are outlined with self-adhesive gold rickrack. Then tiny flat-back angels are glued to the center of the four sides. The top is then decorated with various size beads and gold cord secured through cap at top of cube. A third cube is sprayed silver with beads glued in a solid pattern to the four sides and centered with a tiny pearl-like medallion. The top and bottom are decorated with larger pearls in a rather formal design. The fourth cube has the same geometric design of pearls, sequins and gold glitter flakes repeated on all sides and bottom. A tiny madonna is glued to the cap at top of cube, surrounded by another geometric pattern of various sized pearls and tiny translucent seed beads.

To place the decoration inside a cube, use a sharp knife and cut very carefully along top edge at cap line to remove center structure which will lift from cube. Cut or pull out the center bulbs and wires from the cap or lid. Remove foil reflector and decorate the four concave sections of reflector as desired. Replace decorated reflector in cube. Glue cap to top of cube and decorate outside with braids, beads, etc.

Decorate one side of cube and allow it to dry before starting on the next side. For an unusual effect, fill some cubes with broken tree ornaments which have been crushed. Others can be filled with beads, crystal clear crushed glass or stones. Scenes can be created inside the cube with groups of tiny figurines. Here is a discard that offers an almost unlimited challenge to your imagination and talents.

The decorated cubes shown are from a large collection designed by a friend, Mrs. Mark Keller of Dixon, Illinois.

An old rusty feed store scoop was cleaned, painted black with a red handle. A Styrofoam base was secured to the flat side of the scoop and permanent pine with bright red and green vegetables arranged in Styrofoam and a ruby red glass peg light added to brighten a kitchen or family room.

A lantern made from a milk carton is a conversation piece and is especially good for table decorations where the budget is limited. The design is penciled on the carton and cut out with a sharp knife or razor blade. I use a metal straightedge for clean, sharp lines. Invert a margarine container and glue this to the bottom of milk container. Spray with flat black floral spray. Make or buy a small candle ring of permanent holiday foliages to encircle the hobnail vigil light, then add a decorative spray to the top. The Christmas decorations can be removed and various decoratives added for other seasons.

My crowbar was used to remove the front leg of an outcast upholstered chair. Now it is used as a base for a candle. The velvet ribbon around the base covers the grooves of the chair frame. The leg was refinished and a disk of Styrofoam, secured with glue or floral clay, was impaled on three finishing nails spaced in a circle on top of the inverted chair leg. A peg light is secured to center of Styrofoam. Pine and fruit are picked into Styrofoam with small loops of antique gold tubing added for a touch of elegance.

These porcelain-like flowers are made from throw-away plastic spoons. Hold a plastic spoon over a lighted candle (not too close!) until handle bends to a right angle just below cup of spoon. Allow to firm. Holding a spoon cup over the candle, keep turning the spoon until desired shape is attained. Break second spoon at handle, hold spoon cup with pliers over heat and repeat the process for the second petal. Repeat the same process with handle. Make several petals from spoon cups and spoon handles before assembling flowers. To attach petals to form a flower, hold stem end of individual petals over flame until soft and press in place to weld. This welding method adheres without the use of glue. For flower center use small broken pieces of spoon handles, hold over flame with pliers, and keep turning until desired curved shape is achieved. Weld in place. Now you have a finished flower with a stem. Use handle as stem to insert in Styrofoam base. For a longer stem attach a florist wood pick to handle and bind stem and pick with white floratape. Arrange in container with permanent foliages to create an attractive design for the table.

Miniature bird feeder decorations made from pill containers can be a welcome addition to the family Christmas tree. Larger container lids are decorated and glued to the bottom of the pill container for a tray to which bird seed is glued. Pill container is filled two-thirds with bird seed and capped. A cardboard roof is trimmed and glued to the top. Decorative birds are secured to a perch which has been glued to the side of the container.

The birdhouse decoration with the checked ribbon trim is a discarded juice container covered with a colored burlap ribbon. Cut a hole, then trim as desired. Insert perch in a punched hole and add a perky little bird. The other birdhouse decoration shown in the photo is a covered Bufferin container with a Contac paper roof.

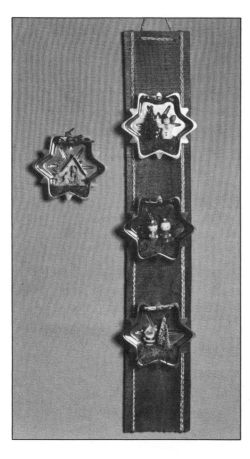

The salad molds were closeouts at a sidewalk sale. Decorate with little figurines mounted on moss-covered Styrofoam secured in the mold. Molds are glued to a stained and braid-trimmed crate board. The star mold is a perfect foil for the tiny Nativity figurines.

Caps from Micrin mouthwash bottles are lined in the center with red felt, then glued to a red felt-covered cardboard. Polka dot ribbon trim is repeated in outer circle of cap and along edge of cardboard. Small figurines are secured to the center circle of cap. The hanger is made of red yarn.

The roof on the open plastic egg is made from throwaway ice-cream bar sticks, glued onto light cardboard. The ridge is glued to act as a hinge, so the roof can be raised or flattened.

Outmoded, discarded jewelry and trimmings are right at home on this cutout wall tree. Heavy cardboard is cut to pattern and layered with cotton before covering with white felt. Felt is sewed along the outer edge to the cardboard. Metallic gold eyelash tubing is glued along the edge and draped across the center. A set of twenty tiny clear tree lights are inserted from the back through X-shaped slits made in the cardboard, cotton and felt. Any excess electric cord is taped to back of design. Metallic gold bow is added to base. Jewelry and other trinkets are pinned or glued to felt.

Ham cans can be painted or covered with cloth to form a créche for the nativity scene. Gold-sprayed Styrofoam is cut to form a base and the figurines secured in place by florist clay or glue. Small, gold-sprayed palmetto leaf is in the background and decorative ribbons and tubing trim the sharp edges of the can. The hanger loop is secured with an adhesive.

Empty plastic pill containers retrieved from the medicine cabinet offer limitless possibilities for designs. Place upright on a foil-covered cookie sheet in a preheated 450° oven. In a few minutes they will melt into random forms and shapes. The longer they are in the hot oven the flatter they become. Press an interesting decorative object into the soft mass as soon as it is removed from the oven and with an ice pick, punch a hole for hanging. Additional decoratives can be added after cooling. Practice with a couple of containers so you will know what to expect.

POTPOURRI

This section is devoted to a variety of designs that you may want to include in your decorating plans. In this instance the word potpourri is used as a blend of color, texture and designs.

On page 58 I have shown three more mantels which are described below. A permanent pine garland is draped around the heavy gold frame of the colonial portrait. Norway spruce cones sprayed with gold paint are at the top center and the corners repeating the color of the gold frame and brass accessories. A low bowl of Filfast will keep the evergreen Japanese yew fresh for several weeks by adding water daily to the container. The gold Norway spruce cones are repeated in the bowl arrangement. Any additional decoratives would tend to detract from the simplicity of the setting.

A very dear friend gave me this lovely old clock and candlesticks, both brought to Dixon from her old family home in Vermont. She often recalled how these antiques were used when she was a child. I have designed this basket arrangement from her recollections of the flowers they often dried to use at the holidays. The liner in the basket contains a block of Barfast, a base used for holding dried materials. I have used dried variegated holly, red cockscomb, yellow yarrow, goldenrod and magnolia leaves. Long-burning beeswax candles glow in the antique brass candlesticks. This setting was more or less traditional in a colonial home during the 1800's.

The wreath shown on the cover is repeated with a completely different background on page 38. We are showing it again with a garland of permanent pine, being careful not to add anything that might detract from the elegant simplicity of the wreath. The copper coffeepot is arranged with fresh pine and berried cedar in Filfast. Only water added every few days is needed to keep it fresh for many weeks.

Double wreath made of dried materials, mounted on a board which has been covered with velvet ribbon.

ORIENTAL ARRANGEMENT

A Styrofoam disk is adhered to the top of the container and covered with sheet moss. Stem ends are tipped with glue before being inserted into Styrofoam. Natural, dried materials are used in this design—Japanese Fantail Willow, Protea, Italian spiral cones (platysper) and preserved Canaerti juniper.

NUT WREATH

This nut and cone outlined wreath is made on a moss-covered straw wreath base. Jersey cone rosettes outline the outer and inner circle. The nuts and pods include: English and American walnuts, hickory and hickory nut husks, Brazil nuts, Sweet Gum pods, peach pits, acorns and acorn caps, buckeyes and hard buckeye pods. Use whatever interesting pods, nuts and cones that are available in your area.

Wreath of dried pods
and botanicals

POTPOURRI

It is appropriate that we conclude this
section with a recipe for a flower potpourri that
you can prepare in your kitchen.

2 quarts fragrant varieties of rose petals and buds, picked when the sun is on them. Dry on sheets of paper. Sprinkle with salt.

Add (dried) a few other fragrant blossoms such as garden pinks or heliotrope, a few herbs such as rosemary, marjoram, a few balsam needles, a bit more salt.

Remember roses must predominate. When all are thoroughly dried, sift out the salt. Add the following mixture and store in a lightly covered crockery jar for several weeks, stirring occasionally.

1 oz. cloves	3 oz. brown sugar
2 oz. allspice	2 oz. powdered orris root
1 oz. cinnamon	⅛ oz. crushed cardamom seed
½ oz. mace	1 oz. gum benzoin
1 oz. pure alcohol	4 drops of attar of roses or synthetic rose perfume

Place in a container and remove cover to scent the room in the wintertime.

TWELFTH NIGHT
ARRANGEMENT

The same technique is used in making this design as that discussed in the Child's Nativity scene on page 50. Coronation gold yarrow is combined with contorted Japanese Fantail Willow in this Twelfth Night arrangement.

TWELFTH NIGHT

Twelfth Night is that magical night when the Wise Men arrived at the manger in Bethlehem to present royal gifts to the Christ Child. Since the middle of the fourth century this event has been celebrated on January 6th.

Pope Julius I was very interested in chronicling the date of Christ's birth and the subsequent story of the Magi and their gifts. In 353 A. D. Pope Julius I formed a council consisting of church students and historians, astrologers, philosophers and other men of wisdom to determine the date which would be celebrated as the date of Christ's birth. After great deliberation this council set December 25th as the date of Christ's birth and nearly all the churches of the world now adhere to this date. January 6th, which was the date formerly celebrated as Christ's birth, was then commemorated as the anniversary of the baptism of Christ, later celebrated in many lands as Three Kings Day, and eventually termed "Twelfth Night."

Early church artists in their paintings and sculpture depicted two or four wise men. The Bible never mentioned the number of wise men—they were created only in the minds of the artists. Another duty of this papal council was to determine a set number of wise men. Augustine, a member of the council and later to be canonized, favored twelve—symbolic of the twelve tribes of Israel and the twelve apostles. The Pope finally settled on three because Matthew in his account mentioned three gifts. After this papal edict was issued, artists began showing three Wise Men in all their religious paintings and sculptures.

Gradually, over a period of nearly nine hundred years the Wise Men began to take on individuality as each acquired a country of origin and a name. Too, the words "Magi" and "Wise Men" were transformed into "kings". By this time they were now known as kings, and artists began portraying them in the regalia and with the retinue symbolic of kings.

Melchior is now depicted as an old man and always carries a casket of gold, which is a symbol of love.

Balthazar is a mature man identified with Ethiopia and is usually depicted as a Negro. He carries an urn of myrrh, symbol of suffering and sacrifice. Myrrh is a sticky substance from a very thorny shrub and is said to contain healing powers.

Gaspar, a youth, carries a vessel of frankincense. Frankincense is a symbol of prayer. This is a very sweet fragrance derived from a plant and burned as an incense.

It is an interesting and unusual coincidence that these three gifts should be brought to the Christ Child, as they were symbolic of Christ's life during His thirty-three years on earth.

Twelfth Night and its relation to the Three Kings grew along with the centuries until today it is celebrated in many lands in various ways. In many areas it is celebrated with parties as the last day of the Christmas season and, fittingly enough, a time to remove Christmas decorations. "Untrim the tree" parties are becoming popular. Although churches celebrate it as Epiphany, not all churches recognize it as a high church holiday. To most of us it is the end of a joyous season, a time to renew our faith, our hope, our love for the years that lie ahead.

As I close this book I am sure you will realize the importance Christmas has played in my life and the love I have for this beautiful season. May your homes and lives be enriched with more beautiful and meaningful decorations created by your own talents. I hope you have enjoyed reading and studying this book as much as I have enjoyed writing it for you.

Christmas is a season, not a day.
Christmas opens with Advent.
Christmas closes with Twelfth Night.

Thank you and a happy holiday.

ABOUT THE AUTHOR

When other children were looking wistfully through candy-shop windows, Harold Cook was standing outside flower-shop windows, entranced by the beauty he saw there. He recalls his youth and remarks that "for as long as I can remember, I've loved trees, plants, flowers and creating design with natural objects." That is why this book has been written—to give this information to others so that they might also learn to love plants and flowers, and to create beautiful arrangements for many occasions.

A native of Illinois, Harold Cook has an impressive list of accomplishments in the gardening field. He has appeared as guest lecturer for design schools in several states, and at annual garden club conventions. He has appeared as lecturer on his favorite subject at all the major universities and for the design schools of the various state floral associations.

He also directed the flower show that marked the opening of the first McCormick Place in Chicago in 1960 and has continued to contribute his talents to his field through his annual "Day of Christmas" lectures in Dixon, Illinois.

His friendship with Mrs. Charles R. Walgreen of the drugstore family provided the impetus for what became his life's work and his enthusiasm for flowers, plants and design is apparent to the reader of this most interesting and informative book. His shops in Dixon are situated in a natural wooded setting and attract thousands of visitors annually.

IDEALS: America's Most Beautiful and Wholesome Publications

In addition to IDEALS bimonthly issues, we also publish a full line of greeting card booklets, gift books, and hardbound books reflecting themes of friendship, old-fashioned ideals, homey philosophy, inspiration, neighborliness – things many of us may have overlooked during these busy days. Ideal for your own inspirational reading and distinctive gifts for every and all occasions.

To examine and purchase these lovely publications, contact your local bookstore, gift shop, greeting card shop, or stationery store. If not available, contact Ideals Publishing Corp., 11315 Watertown Plank Rd., Milwaukee, WI 53226 to receive our latest catalog or address of your nearest dealer.

Editorial Director, James Kuse
Managing Editor, Ralph Luedtke
Photographic Editor, Gerald Koser